Stephan Hermlin

Evening Light

Translated by Paul F. Dvorak

 Fjord Press   San Francisco   1983

Title of original German edition: *Abendlicht*
Published in German simultaneously by Verlag Klaus Wagenbach,
West Berlin, and Verlag Philipp Reclam jun., Leipzig
Copyright © 1979 Verlag Klaus Wagenbach, West Berlin

Published and distributed by:
Fjord Press
P.O. Box 615
Corte Madera, California 94925

Editors: Steven T. Murray & Susan Doran
Cover design & illustration: Tom Cervenak
Book design & typography: Accent & Alphabet

Library of Congress Cataloging in Publication Data:
Catalog Card No.: 81-71427
Hermlin, Stephan
  Evening light.
San Francisco, CA: Fjord Press
120 p.
8203   811120
ISBN: 0-940242-03-6

Printed in the United States of America
First edition, June 1983
9 8 7 6 5 4 3 2 1

*One could tell by the evening light
on the paths that they were
paths home.*

Robert Walser

Two oboes and an oboe da caccia up front and strings and continuo in the rear begin the theme, which the chorus repeats homophonically from bar 24. A breath of coolness emanates from the woods. How quickly the day has passed. Twilight has set in; from its folds a deeper darkness will fall. Where some raise questions, others will have no answer, and where answers are given, questions will be waiting. With increased tempo a choral fugue begins *alla breve*. Later the alto's voice descends lower and lower in whole notes. Darkness blots out the faces, the traces of the day's work, the brighter colors of the street. No windows gleam any longer, no neighborly house, no community waits. The strings, playing G-D-B-F#, describe a cross. Abide with us.

He must walk toward the sun, we sang, who truly walks in joy. The sun hovered over the eastern crest of the mountains as we crossed the bridge over the Inn River. I stopped on the bridge, right in the middle of the wide, endless valley. For a minute I was deaf to my teachers' calls. In the depths of the swift gray-green waters I thought I caught a glimpse of the schools of trout that inhabited them, and then I saw the mountain that seals off the valley far to the south, the one I used to call my mountain and have never forgotten — La Margna. *Und der Himmel da oben, wie ist er so weit*; how peaceful the sky could be in those days, no vapor trails marked it yet, it drew your gaze upward past the distant mountain and let it fall from depth to depth, for depth was not only below in the waters, it surrounded me on all sides, its other name was tranquility, and nowhere was it deeper than in the blue up above into which I floated, and down into which I sank. As always, my eyes sought out the clouds that wandered as I did, resembling one another as they had for millennia, and yet they were so painfully changeable, showing to me that no future moment would ever be like this one.

The sun grew stronger, it glowed in the eerie blue high above the forests on the slope, in whose shadows I ran here and there, picking Alpine roses and stuffing them into my little knapsack; they would not be damaged, not wilt right away, they were hearty flowers that would continue to blaze in my memory long after I had filled the vases at home with them.

The cuckoo called from the woods, it wasn't necessary to count his calls, life stretched out endlessly before me. The day arched higher, only rarely were people visible, yet everywhere their quiet, friendly presence could be sensed in the solid, centuries-old houses, in the clean streets through which a wagon sometimes creaked; far off a shepherd rested on his staff next to the larches. Every hour the electric-powered train passed through the valley; its rolling and rushing sound quickly faded.

Later in the afternoon, with school and my midday nap behind me, I walked past the house of the Plantas, through the meadows, downstream toward the needle spire of the church in Scanf. Awaiting me there was the old pastor, who read Cornelius Nepos with me. A wall clock ticked slowly and steadily. Enveloped in the warm light that fell on my book in a column of dancing dust and tobacco smoke, I sleepily and contentedly followed the pastor's grammatical explanations. On the way home I lingered near the peasants standing in groups on the village street. I tried not to appear overly curious as I listened to the sounds of their Ladino or German speech; once in a while someone or other cast an impassive, gentle look in my direction. I observed the peasants' powerful frames, their broad dark hands. I understood only part of what they said. On Sundays they would stand in their best clothes beside the church; the women would wear the gold-trimmed black and red costume of the region. These people filled me with diffidence; they were masters over the fields, the meadows, the Alpine pastures, the animals; as the seasons changed, they always knew from one day to the next what had to be done, their paths through the valley, their lingering in this place or that, formed the lines and points of a diagram, a pattern. They knew something unknown to me, something I wanted to know.

But once again my eyes were drawn upward. One shade of blue towered unfathomably over another, a reddish glow forced its way over the peaks to the west. The first pale stars appeared between the sharp contours of the small clouds, and, looking back over my shoulder with dread, I saw the evening eagle high above inscribing circles over the dark triangle of Piz d'Esan.

This slow, groping recovery of one's own body, of the place, of the season, of the approximate hour. What really was it . . . Through a window three stars, sparkling coldly, become visible. It is winter, but just a moment ago there was a warmth, no, more than that, radiant heat — desert-like, parching, stifling. I was on the open sea, actually over it, for I was flying, though no sound could be heard, in a craft I could not see yet was able to steer. I was flying over an almost motionless, leaden, biblical sea, like the one I had seen decades ago during a flood on the island of Föhr. My craft flew quickly, it was perfectly responsive, in an instant I could swoop down from an astronaut's height and dart right along the surface of the water.

All this immobility below me, or rather this slow, scarcely perceptible, languid breathing of the waters in a light that comes from nowhere. The winds are calm. No coast, no island, no ship. But something tells me I must be over the Channel, approximately at the point where it leads into the North Sea. How can it be then that I can see nothing of Harwich, of Holland? Perhaps I am really much farther west over the open sea. Just now I can see something from my very high vantage point, a boat perhaps, or a plank, in any case something is bobbing up and down with the sluggish rhythm of the water, and when I descend lower, it is the wing of an airplane, it is, as I now clearly realize, the wing of a Spitfire, and lying across it is a man on his back; I suspect what is coming, and a moment later I see my brother. He is lying right next to the roundel insignia, he is wearing his Mae West and his aviator's cap with headset, his pale face is somewhat bloated, but almost as it had been in life, and when I descend even more, I see that he has something white in one hand, a sheet of paper, a note. I immediately climb higher again—one ought to get help, or rather, have his body recovered so he can be properly buried, so his squadron can fire its salute of honor. Strangely enough, however, I turn east instead of west. Already there is land below me, I can clearly make out the coastline of the continent, I've become an astronaut again, no clouds block my view, once again I sense the heat that surrounds me, now there's a burnt smell too, is it possible that the forests below me are burning? I'm flying very low again, I almost brush the treetops, nothing is burning, there's no movement at all, even though part of the time I'm flying over cities and villages half or totally destroyed, but those fires down below have long since been extinguished. No one is in sight, I fly over the sluggish rivers that move northward between flat banks, I fly over huge, freshly plowed fields, then again over clusters of long, single-story buildings, are they barracks, huts; once in a while tall, slender smokestacks come into view next to workshops, but no one is there, no human being, no movement, everything is mired in this dead, viscous heat. In a wide arc I turn again to the west, far off the sea emerges, the dead pilot is still bobbing up and down on the wing, unchanged, he is still holding the white sheet of paper in his hand, something is written on it, I fly lower to read what it says, it's not a note, it's a page from a calendar showing the date of June 22nd, and at this moment a howling starts up all around me, it is, as I realize only later, the sound of my own screaming, for the calendar page, or rather the power that has pressed it into my brother's hand, makes it clear that this date has been eradicated from time, this day does not exist, it will never again exist, there is only June 21st, followed by June 23rd, and the 23rd will be as the 21st was, it's been arranged that way, and from now on all days will succeed one another without change, in this hush, this windless calm, this glowing heat, this languid rocking of the waters beneath a light not born of day.

13

The years in the mountains were not easy for me. Having been alone for so long, I adjusted slowly to the new children. I missed my tutors, my governess, the maids, all the people who had surrounded me every day before I came to the boarding school. Unchanging, they had stood around me, full of inscrutable wisdom and experience, always looking after me, sometimes insisting adamantly on some demand, but always friendly and bestowing trust. I didn't see my parents the entire time. Only once did they appear, youthful and radiant, they had been traveling in Italy, now they took me along to the Suvretta House, we ate among total strangers. The next day was the national holiday, after it got dark, fires shone forth from the mountaintops, we had to sing in front of the hotel guests in the lobby, I saw my parents in evening attire among other splendidly dressed guests, we sang *In Sempach der kleinen Stadt*. In an amusing way we had become patriotic at the boarding school, even though all of us students were foreigners, and then my parents rushed off and I didn't see them again until much later.

We were educated well according to modern principles, and I had even begun to like the teachers, though all of them could not replace the absent, familiar people. Most of all I loved Fräulein Zehnder. Once she was sitting talking with some other teachers, while I stood unsuspectingly nearby, there was something serious, even sad in their faces. Fräulein Zehnder suddenly turned toward me and said: "How old am I, what do you think? . . ." They all looked expectantly at me. It was difficult for me to guess the age of grownups, it was something intangible; I hesitated. "The teachers' college has spent our youth," Fräulein Zehnder said softly. For the first time I vaguely sensed there were such things as missed opportunity, failure, regret in this world.

Attending Sunday school was my greatest joy. We learned the beautiful chorales of Paul Gerhardt, we heard stories from the New Testament that we had to retell. When we learned something well, we were rewarded with little pictures showing episodes from the Bible. Suddenly these colorful, garish pictures seemed to me the most beautiful things I had ever seen; they were much more beautiful than the paintings that had surrounded me at home. I dreamed all week long of those I would get the following Sunday. I would sit in my small attic room on Sunday afternoon and look at these pictures that delighted me so, I saw the city of Emmaus in the distance, and Cleophas in the foreground, meeting Christ. Under the picture were the words: Abide with us, for it will soon be evening, and day is nearly done.

To our delight winter lasted a long time. It began in October and ended in April. The snow was so deep that the janitor often had to shovel the house door free. We were encouraged to ski, which most of us enjoyed and did with increasing skill. Several of the older boys had sleds, and we would gaze after them for a long time when they went to Cresta Run.

Evenings I would read *Oliver Twist* in bed, carefully shielding the candle so that the teachers wouldn't see the light under the door during their rounds. Then I would lie a while in the dark, look out from my warm room into the icy night with its huge stars, and think about Oliver Twist's fate. A strong compassion for poor children, who fortunately only existed in books, came over me. Those nights were almost soundless, only seldom pierced by the whistle of a train from the valley. Then spring came, and the frozen waterfalls began to rush again in the glens. Avalanches thundered into my sleep the whole night long. When I awoke, blue and yellow crocuses covered the meadows up to where the bare rock began. It was a beautiful sight, but it struck me like a sharp pain. I had become part of a winter world, of a uniform whiteness in which all otherwise contradictory things came to rest, and above which the sky turned a deeper blue and the stillness was interrupted but not disturbed by those near and distant voices that wandered, echoing and clear, down the valley.

Among my early experiences as a reader, two have become memorable to me for entirely different reasons. The first relates to a book, or several books, I read very early, between the ages of six and eight. I'm thinking of *A Thousand and One Nights*, but Andersen's *Picture Book Without Pictures* appears alongside it, and so do the Leatherstocking tales. That the boundaries, the contours of these very different works become obscured, that they tend to blend into one another, must be because the characters and actions portrayed were not all that important to me. What was important was an imagined landscape, a time of day, an aura in which people moved and acted.

The tendency to place atmosphere above the actual story or, as one might say, to read into a given text a second, different one, was encouraged by the accompanying illustrations, whose creators I have forgotten, if I ever knew them at all. In my edition of *Grimms' Fairy Tales*, which I read constantly, there was the picture of a rising meadow slope, above which was a pale blue sky dappled with white clouds. The fairy-tale characters climbed the meadow slope and lay down upon it in a soundless quietude I longed for. As an adult I visited several Oriental cities (Baghdad was not among them), and everywhere I searched for the alleys and bazaars where a genial and mysterious life slowly passed by. Since the first time I had read *A Thousand and One Nights*, the same ruby glow filtered out from the night of the bazaars, the same little water vendor ran through the heavily cast shadows, the same invisible sun stood against a deep blue sky over the morning coolness in the narrow canyons of the streets. Surrounded by poverty and decay and by the onslaught of a repugnant technology, I stood for a long while next to the storytellers on the streetcorners. I did not understand their language; it was only in the eyes of their ragged listeners that the images and characters of my childhood lived. For a long time I sought a light that I had once seen clearly. I did not find it.

At the age of thirteen I happened to read the *Communist Manifesto*. Later it had its consequences. What first fascinated me about the work was its grand poetic style, then the logic of what was said. One consequence was that I read it repeatedly, certainly two dozen times over the years. In three countries I listened to my teacher, Hermann Duncker, lecture on the Manifesto; Duncker, who could have recited the work from the first to the last word by heart, was one of those no longer living who still spoke about Marxist theory with tears of emotion. This famous work led me to more difficult

and more voluminous writings of Marxist literature, but I returned to it again and again. I had long
thought I knew the work well when, at about the
age of fifty, I made a striking discovery. Among the
sentences which I had for a long time taken for
granted was one which went as follows: "In place of
the old bourgeois society, with its classes and class
antagonisms, we shall have an association in which
the free development of all is the condition for the
free development of each." I don't know when I
began to read the sentence the way it's written
here. I read it that way, it sounded that way to me,
because that was the way it corresponded to my
understanding of the world at that time. How great
was my surprise, indeed my horror, when I found
out after many years that the sentence actually said
just the opposite: " . . . in which the free development of each is the condition for the free development of all."

It was clear to me that here as well, to some
extent, I had read into a text a different text, my
own point of view, my own immaturity; but it was
also clear that what was formerly permitted and
even required, because this phrase implied other
phrases and not yet articulated ideas, now became
absurd, since in my own mind a perception, a

prophecy, had been stood on its head. Still, my horror was mixed with relief. Suddenly a text had appeared before my eyes that I had long awaited, had hoped for.

My relatives didn't interest me, I didn't love any of them except Uncle Herbert, who was my father's younger brother. Uncle Herbert seldom visited. He would show up only two or three times a year, always accompanied by a powerful Newfoundland, black and quiet, that took its usual position in the hall. My brother and I let out a shout of joy at our uncle's arrival, for he always brought along beautiful books for us, or a mechanical toy like nothing we had ever seen. We laughed at his black, broad-brimmed hat. Our uncle smiled back at us good-naturedly. Sometimes the artist S., whose enticing paintings in gray and blue-gray hues my father admired, came along with him. S. would then stay for several days as well. The house was large and we often had guests.

My father was not one to make a demonstrative show of his pleasure, but joy positively radiated from him whenever Uncle Herbert came to visit us. My uncle resembled my father, he too was of medium height and had the same blue eyes, but he was broader, he tended to be a little stout, and there was a trace of weakness in his smile. Whenever he came, my mother, who was seldom at home, seemed to be even busier than usual — she would start mentioning the magical names of the milliner Gerson, of the jeweler Markus, of the hairdresser

Karsten. As soon as Uncle Herbert had freshened up a little, my father and he would close themselves off for a while in the study. No sound could be heard from within. When both of them reappeared, they sat down at the piano and played Schubert's *Fantasia in F minor* and other pieces for four hands. I had the impression that by making music, or rather through music, they were continuing their conversation. Uncle Herbert played just as well as my father. Whenever my father was not at home, Uncle Herbert would play alone. He always produced a thick stack of music from his luggage; he played composers we otherwise would not be able to hear, rather new composers such as Scriabin, Ravel, and an Englishman named Cyrill Scott. While he played, I watched his hands, the fingers yellowed from smoking. Both brothers were heavy smokers, often they even smoked at the piano, but Uncle Herbert's cigarettes were much different from my father's, they had a peculiar sweet smell. Sometimes my uncle would quietly enter the music room when I was practicing. He would listen to me a while and then praise my progress. I discovered that he also knew something about playing the violin; he corrected the way I held my chin and left hand to improve my vibrato.

I never heard him raise his voice, I never saw

anything in his manner that wasn't kindness and love. Once I asked him a question; the barely perceptible effect it had on Uncle Herbert unsettled me. Since he had usually come to us by himself or with S., I asked him whether he was really all alone, whether he wasn't married. With his familiar but now somewhat contorted smile, Uncle Herbert said he wasn't. He stroked my hair and sat down at the piano.

I noticed that the servants treated Uncle Herbert with a somewhat exaggerated politeness, as if they were secretly making fun of him. He didn't seem to notice, he would thank them softly when they offered a hand or a bit of information; I saw that he cast his eyes down as he did so.

Once I told my governess I loved Uncle Herbert as much as I did my father. She pressed her lips together and cast a hard look at the wall. "Your uncle is kind and good," she said coldly after a while, "but he's not fit for life." I wanted to know what that was supposed to mean. "All he can do is play the piano and spend money that's not his own. The Master"—she never referred to my father and mother other than as "Master" and "Mistress"— "the Master keeps him, he pays everything for him, it's really a shame, your uncle is like a child . . .

He's not to be compared with the Master. And anyway . . ." With this puzzling "and anyway" she ended her lecture, which made little impression on me. I felt that I loved Uncle Herbert even more now because according to her he was like a child.

At about this time I became an unwilling witness to an argument between my parents. I would have paid no attention to it had it not involved Uncle Herbert, as I soon guessed. I was sitting on the floor in the corner of one room with a book in front of me when my parents entered the next room. They couldn't see me. My mother was talking insistently to my father, who had dropped himself heavily into an armchair. "You could show some consideration for once," I heard my mother say. "People like him are rather unreliable, you know." As was occasionally her somewhat silly habit, she repeated the sentence in English. "Please, no more," I heard my father say softly, "no more now, please." I tiptoed out of the room without their noticing me.

I must have been nine years old, and it had been many months since Uncle Herbert had visited us, when some commotion erupted in the house during one of my lessons. I heard running back and forth, a door slammed, I could hear muffled talking and lamenting. I ran out of the room, pursued by the commands and protests of my tutor. With eyes red from crying, my governess met me in the hall; she cried at every available opportunity. "Your Uncle Herbert is dead," she whispered, "what a tragedy . . ." I sneaked to my father's study and opened the door quietly. My father, his face pale, stood in the middle of the room looking blindly in my direction.

Somewhere in another country, Uncle Herbert had shot himself. My father went to his funeral. Uncle Herbert was no longer spoken of and was gradually forgotten, even by me. Only sometimes, later on, in the twilight, when I sat alone in the empty music room, did the strange music that arose under his invisible hands still make its way to me.

I ncapable of moving, I lay in the darkness. It was not as before when I ran and felt my legs get heavier and my steps slower, as the invisible pursuers came closer. I was lying on my back, unshackled but rigid, as if I had neither muscles nor sinews, nor could I hear any footsteps around me, only an almost inaudible gliding, creeping, sliding, pushing, and the shadow of incomprehensible words, softer than a whisper. There was no persecution here, they had caught up with me long ago, I was at their mercy, invisible glances glided over me, they were observing, appraising me, they were going to do something with me, only they had not agreed on the time or on the operation they were planning. For it had to be some kind of operation, the thought became certainty in an instant, they did not want to tolerate me any longer as I was, I was supposed to become someone else, I would be exchanged like a piece of worn-out metal, I heard a voice: "Je est un autre." Was it a quote or was it the voice of Rimbaud himself? They would give me new senses, new reflexes, new feelings, whatever was sharp in me they would blunt, where I was tough they would make me pliable, where I was compassionate they would make me hard. I cried out, I heard myself ask: "Where am I?" and heard the incomprehensible, enigmatic reply in me or outside me: "Under a chemical coat."

In the summer of 1931 on my daily walk to school, a small group of people in front of the windows of a newsstand caught my eye. I walked up to them and stopped a while, noticing that they were involved in a political discussion. Hanging side by side in the windows were the front pages of the Berlin newspapers, from the National Socialist *Angriff* to the Communist *Rote Fahne*. The men in the group were unemployed; the meager support they received did not allow most of them to buy a daily newspaper; here through the panes of the newsstand they could at least read the most important news.

It became a habit for me to stop every day at this spot and follow the conversations, which sometimes became heated. The frantic, consuming interest in political events had gripped me too. I could easily see that the debaters could be divided into three categories: there were Social Democrats, Communists, and National Socialists; no other points of view were represented. At home everyone began to wonder: I was always late for dinner. I made excuses by pretending to need more time for sports and for a group project at school.

Almost all those men who spent their time in front of the newsstand were laborers or minor clerks, they were hardly interested in what had interested me up to that time, they knew nothing about it, but I felt that they knew many things that had remained hidden from me. It never occurred to me to take part in their conversations. For several weeks I remained a silent listener.

I noticed that the Social Democrats and Communists, even if they continuously cast ironic or spiteful remarks at one another, were reasonably united against the National Socialists. Of the arguments the three groups advanced, those of the Communists were most convincing to me. I also liked the Communists I saw daily. Although they were obviously having a hard time, they had a certain enthusiasm and confidence.

I felt myself turn pale when one of them suddenly spoke to me one day. It was only a few days before the beginning of summer vacation. To be sure, I had occasionally been the recipient of indifferent or well-intentioned looks before, but now someone was coming up to me, two pale blue eyes looked me right in the face and a voice said: "So, what are you . . . I bet you're a high-school student, right?" The voice sounded ironic but in no way hostile; it had a metallic ring, not like the sound of a precious metal, more like the rattle of sheet metal. You could tell this person had no intention of being fooled, the voice was alert, without illusion, brave, not pleasing. I loved the voices of Berlin, there was melancholy in them too, a melancholy that does not like to admit it exists. At the moment the stranger spoke to me, resentment over his sudden and casual familiarity struggled with a puzzling joy within me. I supplied information about myself, yes, I attend this and that school, I live here and there, I am against the fascists. We exchanged a few more words before the stranger suddenly asked me: "Well, what do you say — do you want to join us?" He had pulled a wrinkled, not very clean slip of paper from his jacket pocket and held it out to me. It was not printed, it had been produced on a mimeograph machine, and it stated in washed-out, pale letters that the undersigned was from now on a member of the Communist Youth Association of Germany. In those days a person could join up on the street, no references or candidacies were needed, and the new comrade was not handed any flowers. I had never been in a political organization before; I belonged to no sports or hiking club. I looked at the wrinkled, smeared piece of paper and signed. The street revolved slowly and incessantly around me.

At that time I didn't know all that I was signing: the duty to fight in a united front with the oppressed, to be treated as an enemy by many who had been close to me, to be unwavering, cold-blooded, discreet, to learn and to pass on what was learned, to endure various sorts of tests, to hold meaning higher than words.

Since then I have often had to ask myself why I remained true to this signature on an ordinary slip of paper, when I saw so many people around me either withdraw their signatures or simply forget them. I too experienced moments when a voice that sounded like the voice of reason tried to persuade me: Could this signature still be valid when the good intentions that resided in it had been so often disappointed? Was I, could I in any way be the same person who signed at that time? But another voice rose up stubbornly against the first: The struggle of the oppressed is the struggle of the oppressed, even if arrogance and conceit, contempt and persistent errors have become apparent recently; the struggle leads to new oppressions, even to crimes; it goes on forever, but it also bears the noble seal of a striving toward humanity, toward freedom and equality for all. At the same time I sensed that I would have to give up the best that was in me, if I ever were to consider the signature I endorsed around noon on a day like many days, in a street like many streets in Berlin, as no longer valid.

At the age of seven I went on a trip with my mother, it was the only time I ever traveled alone with her. One day I felt a vague pain and began to limp, our family doctor spoke about the possibility of tuberculosis of the hip, it was only a suspicion, he said, but he advised that I be taken to the sanatorium of Professor Weidner in Loschwitz near Dresden. A glorious summer arched over the house, where we had an apartment with a large veranda. Several doctors under the direction of the professor examined me thoroughly. I was X-rayed, no, there was no cause for alarm, they said, they would be able to tell, and it would be all right.

My mother went out a lot. She met acquaintances in Dresden who came from Berlin and from other countries, but she was back with me for lunch. Young, elegant men appeared for short visits, they spoke politely with my mother and solicitously with me and soon took their leave. Every morning the maid brought a tray with a few calling cards, my mother read them and laughed playfully, and our rooms filled up with flowers, whole baskets of them were delivered, we hardly noticed them wilt, for new ones soon took their place. My father came once, he kissed me and asked me how I was, he joked with my mother about the flowers and about the young men, but that did not detain him long, he couldn't play the piano here, and in Berlin, as he said, a Herr Bleichröder was expecting him for a meeting. He had brought along our coachman Heinrich with the black carriage and coach horses so that my mother could travel about.

Professor Weidner, a large red-faced man with white hair who dressed in a white smock, appeared regularly for supper on the veranda; he stayed a while with us and had a delicate way of putting a tiny piece of butter on every radish for me and hand-feeding me. Most enjoyable was breakfast, which we usually ate on the veranda as well, but sometimes we had it on the lawn beneath our windows, where many acquaintances would gather at a large table under sunshades. I would step carefully on the crunching gravel, the young men wore ascots of shot silk and tennis pants, my mother's laugh rang clearly, she had the reddish-blond hair and clear complexion of her homeland, I sat between her and the actress Pola Negri, whose fur-lined slippers I admired.

But most of all I liked to lie in my room and read. I had brought along many books, Andersen and little Peter's trip to the moon and the reveries beside a French fireplace. But I was already a newspaper reader too. Every day the *BZ am Mittag*, which had the most extensive sports section of any German newspaper, was brought to me, for I was interested in sports and was encouraged in this by my father, who had already taken me along to boxing matches and six-day bicycle races. Occasionally an inadvertent glance would fall on the political pages of the newspaper as I quickly leafed through it. But on one of those summer days my attention was riveted by a screaming headline on the front page: the foreign minister, Walther Rathenau, had been murdered. Naturally I didn't grasp the significance of this event; I didn't even know what a foreign minister was. But for a time that was all I heard being discussed around me. Up to that point I had perceived violent acts in an almost mild, innocuous way, because they had always belonged to the world of my books, a world that knew how to set things right in the end, so that everything terrible eventually lost its terror. But now I sensed that something had happened in the real world, something irremediable — right before the gates that had protected me so securely from the dangers of life. A remark I heard at the time, that my father had actually known this Rathenau, even if only fleetingly, contributed to my growing anxiety; the dead man was somehow linked to me. For the first time the shadow of a reality I had never before imagined had fallen on me.

In the days that followed I read more about the assassination and its repercussions: the workers had declared a general strike, the police were tracking down the murderers, who were officers in the military. They cornered them in a castle somewhere in central Germany, where the assassins put up a struggle and finally killed themselves. Shortly before this conclusion my anxiety had increased so much that one day, when my mother was away again, I had a screaming fit: I saw before me the country, the cities filled with masked murderers, and I was sure that my mother had fallen into their hands. The doctors and nurses who rushed in were unable to calm me; only my mother managed to do so when she returned soon after.

The foreign minister was buried; the murderers and their accomplices were either dead or under arrest; the green and gold of summer arched anew above the conversations of our friends, above my mother's laughter. What did it matter that I didn't have her alone to myself, that there were always others around us? Dressed in my white sailor suit, I felt a sweet, soporific boredom as I rocked my chair on the gravel. Nothing could happen, nothing could happen to me, no one wished me harm, how kind grownups were and how smart, how well they knew their way about in a world that was inscrutable to me. There was always bread and milk standing there for me, my violin would always be waiting, or a book, or my bed when I was tired. Someone would bring me what I needed, someone would help me get dressed, someone would ask me my lessons, that was all there was, that was life, it made me tired and happy. I let my head sink back, high above me the clouds were dissolving and would never again be exactly the same as at this moment. We would travel back to Berlin, there would be hours like this there too, when my mother, though it seldom happened, would take me along to the Hotel Esplanade to show me to her acquaintances, there too this buzzing would surround me, bees and wasps over the cake plates, this buzzing of friendly voices, there too I would listen without distaste to the band and the awful portamenti of the first violinist, except the distant noises from Potsdamer Platz would be added, the clouds in the sky, and the clouds on the inside of my eyelids. I was almost back to normal now, I was fully recovered, one morning the pain was gone as suddenly as it had come, I ran and jumped as before, and the pain never came back again, it had nothing to do with tuberculosis, Professor Weidner had been right.

I was healthy and went back again with my mother and Heinrich and the horses to the north of this Republic, which was already dying before it had really begun to live.

From the moment I had begun to read Marx and Lenin and joined the workers' movement, I was troubled by the fact that although for me the theory proved its validity, more and more, so far as it concerned general human affairs, I could find nothing comparable in the area of art interpretation. In the classics of Marxism I found important and sometimes dazzling comments on artistic matters, though often they were written not for the sake of art but to shed a clearer light on economic developments. But even their immediate successors had done scarcely anything with these insights. The texts were treated as Holy Writ; they were quoted, whereas real work with them should have treated these insights scientifically, that is, by constantly questioning them anew and in relation to historical developments. To my surprise I discovered in myself a bent toward theory, which was, however, entirely passive and receptive; it never entered my mind to want to make any contribution of my own toward the development of a new aesthetics. Despite my accumulation of a stack of sociological works on art, which soon amounted to a small library, these works appealed to me less and less for I was unable to arrive at any agreement with them and became irritated instead. Because of this I increasingly developed anxieties that I carried around inside me for years, for decades, without being able to speak to anyone about them. There were moments, especially when I had important, even dangerous tasks to accomplish, when I saw myself as lost, as unworthy, as one who, unlike his comrades, was not able to acknowledge and embrace the simple, generally accepted truth. This came about as new exegetes were at work trying to outdo each other with condemnations and newly devised restrictions. The art of this century became more and more a slough of perdition; the great names of literature, music, and painting were made to personify all sorts of evils; third-rate academic epigones were promoted to geniuses. Theorists sought the root causes of this ruin; one zealot had already worked back so far that he was able to declare Flaubert and Baudelaire decadent. Theories and concepts were formed out of thin air; they could not be substantiated, but people acted as if they had long been proven. The word "scientific" was bandied about, but things had already gone further, organized structures had developed: lectures, seminars, departments, newspapers, conferences, academies. Professors taught and students became professors, and we waited in vain for the child from the Andersen fairy tale who cried out: "But the Emperor has no clothes on!"

I am exaggerating here. The chimeras still live on, but they have aged, and fewer and fewer contemporaries still consider them obligatory. I cannot say when my anxieties waned, when they entirely disappeared. I certainly cannot take the entire credit for the knowledge that I am free of them today. The workers' movement has considerable regenerative power, which has also played a role for me, and in me. Yet as I considered the past, I could not overlook the fact that this vain struggle to reach a totally undesirable agreement on an incorrectly stated question had cost me a lot of energy in thirty years and perhaps had hindered me from giving more and better things of myself. I recognized this possibility with no trace of self-pity. I was no better or worse than the movement to which I belonged, I shared its maturity and immaturity, its greatness and its misery. What still isolated me would unite those to come.

One day as a child, sitting as usual next to my governess at the far end of the long table, I noticed an unfamiliar gentleman speaking animatedly to my father during the meal. He had attracted my attention only because of his foreign accent. My father listened to him politely and with raised eyebrows. As usual I didn't say a word, since I knew children were not to interrupt the conversation of adults at the table. I likewise paid no attention to what was said since it was not meant for my ears and did not interest me. After the meal, when the stranger had taken his leave, my father told me this man was a Russian, a famous painter named Kandinsky. "He'd like to sell me a painting," my father said, "but I don't like his paintings. I don't like them because I don't understand them." There were moments when my father, quietly and dreamily, spoke earnestly to me in this way, as if he had not the slightest doubt that I understood him. "Well, what's that supposed to mean," he continued after a while, "what does liking or not liking mean in art? I think he is a great master. You often can't judge works of art. You must be able to wait. Maybe I'll understand Kandinsky some day. You have to have a reverence for art . . ." Later he took me to the Kronprinzenpalais to show me the works of Kandinsky that were there.

Once in a while Father would call me to the graphics cabinets in the largest room of the house where all those many works he had not been able to hang on the walls lay nicely arranged. Even though he owned many other things, above all my father collected the German masters from the early 19th century. He showed me a detail from a sketch by Caspar David Friedrich, a print by Runge, a manneristic study by Blechen. Only rarely did he utter a faint word. I always sensed his trust in my readiness to understand him and to comprehend the artists he let me see. Nothing but tranquility, admiration, and happiness enveloped us; a beautiful, subdued light shone through the windowpanes. Today I know that his few words, his calling attention to this or showing me that, held something more important for me than the sophisms with which I later grappled for far too long. His silence taught me tolerance. But we were living in intolerant times.

It must certainly have been seven years since I had thought about my former friend, Erich M. Seven years before, I had seen him for the last time and then had quickly forgotten him. He was the youngest son of a working-class family, in whose one-room apartment I sat as often as possible. In those days I spent a lot of time in one-room apartments in Berlin. I met new people who intimidated me, though they were not unfriendly; to me they seemed full of secrets, even if they were only talking of everyday matters. Erich's father had fought with the Spartacists; he seldom spoke, looked exhausted and, as Erich said, "had it in the lungs." Both of Erich's brothers worked as specialists in the Soviet Union, at Elektrozavod. It was the era of the first five-year plan. With quiet enthusiasm, I looked at the pictures in magazines of the new cities Le Corbusier and Ernst May were building. Every week I read Karl Radek's *Moskauer Rundschau*, which was printed on poor paper but written in good German. Whenever Erich's brothers happened to be spending some time off in Berlin, I would persuade them to visit my group. How good those evenings were— we would look forward to them for a long time, could hardly wait for them. Everyone would give each other a warm welcome. Almost all my comrades were young and unemployed. Many of the young people had gone straight from vocational school to the employment office, which they could not get free of. They hung around in front of it; it had no jobs to offer them.

For a while I remained an outsider; I received either suspicious or ironic looks. Then I proved myself. It was a time of latent civil war, and I had not backed off from the SA or the police. Anyway, it was not the street and meeting-hall battles I feared. The door-to-door agitation unsettled me far more — ringing at strange doors, having to start a conversation with people I had never seen before. I had to struggle against the fears that such encounters caused me. I suppressed them with great difficulty, yet they always came up again. My friends knew nothing about it. They had observed me and now treated me as one of their own.

Whenever Erich's brothers visited us, our enthusiastic curiosity knew no bounds. We never tired of asking them questions. They told us about everyday life in Moscow, about tremendous feats of accomplishment, about need and deprivation, without fear of naming deficiencies by name. They commented on statistics: their plans and counterplans, their food rations. Want and hunger could not diminish the Soviet Union in our eyes; these things were inherited from the past, from a corrupt society, from war and imposed civil war. There was hunger in Germany now too. It was the result of the gluttony of the few. Over there a country that had no unemployed was preparing abundance for everyone. They had their housing shortages, but those cities were already under construction — the ones I called "the white cities" in my dreams and later in a poem because I saw them white and perfect in the photographs in *UdSSR im Bau* and in the *Arbeiter-Illustrierte*. In Germany there were enough apartments, but hundreds of people were evicted daily because they could no longer pay their rent. We laughed about the reports in the bourgeois newspapers of deprivation in Russia; it was an unrestrained laughter, for we knew that there things would pick up quickly, while here at home capitalism was at its end.

It was the beginning of February, only a few days after Hitler seized power, when I heard drums and singing as I walked down a side street of the Kaiserallee. I stopped and a few seconds later saw a squad of Hitler Youth swing into my street singing. In the dubious German of many soldiers' songs they sang:

> So that the Fatherland not pass away,
> They died in an assault near La Bassée.

I had never heard the song before. Even though the years passed, the melody and text remained fixed in my memory, as did the rapid pivoting of the left flank around the corner, and the pivot man in the second row, singing loudly and wearing a brown shirt and a brown cap, was my friend Erich M. He saw me and turned beet-red, and at the same time I felt myself turn pale. He looked straight ahead. It had taken only a few hours or days to transform him in this way. I was seventeen years old and did not understand it, but I learned to understand it long after he had passed. He was the first; I saw countless others follow. The urge to be among the stronger is uncontrollable. On how many battle-fields had those threatened with defeat changed their allegiances.

Seven years and some months had passed since this street scene when I suddenly thought of Erich M., who, as I already mentioned, had totally slipped from my mind. It was night, and we were lying in a hollow after marching almost constantly and in various directions for the past few days. We no longer knew exactly where we were; stragglers joined our unit, and civilians as well, only to vanish as suddenly as they had appeared. We listened for tanks, which could sometimes be heard unexpectedly not far from where we were. During the day the sky was full of their planes, we heard bombs in the distance, a squadron of Morane planes fleeing from a few Messerschmitts, the war dissolved us, dissolved itself, before we had really assimilated it. With an empty gaze I saw a poster on a wall in an empty village: *"Nous vaincrons, parce que nous sommes les plus forts."* Columns of German tanks could appear from anywhere; many, it was said, were advancing from far to the south. The main thrust of the Germans was no longer from the north. They were attacking from Mézières and from the forest of Mormal, that is, from an easterly direction. They advanced to the coast and cut off the British from the French troops. I saw the stars in the sky, the circular beam of a flashlight on a map not far from me. A few officers murmured insistently nearby. It reminded me of my childhood, when I loved to hear the conversations of grownups around me, conversations I did not understand and did not want to understand, whose sound I loved and whose meaning was immaterial to me. From this inaudible conversation only one sentence made its way through my exhaustion: "They've taken Lens, Béthune, and La Bassée," someone said. A monstrous uniformity of history became apparent; every twenty years the same names recurred, which otherwise went unmentioned, again and again the

47

same fate returned like a devouring avalanche, villages and small towns seemed to exist only to be conquered, to be lost, and the lives of suffering people moved toward their future suffering.

A fog that would not disperse made the dark autumn day darker, it grew even heavier in the afternoon as I rode the train to the park. The train did not go any farther, the people didn't seem to expect anything different, most of them got off with me and went in the same direction, no one knew anyone else, but I was one of them, and a vague contentment and well-being filled me. Surrounding me was a surging tide of worn-out jackets and coats, off to the side a cordon of police could be seen protecting the restricted area. At a continually increasing distance were my home, my family, the circle of people among whom I was accustomed to living.

For the first time I took part in a mass demonstration. Individual torches burned in front of the balustrade of the palace. Wilhelm Florin was speaking. I glanced into the drab gray behind the stiff, despairing gestures of the bare branches. Standing in the vicinity of the speaker, I noticed what efforts he made to be heard, for no amplifier reinforced his voice, which, even when raised to a shout, only reached a few yards. Many speakers who survived these times retained the habit of talking in an excessively loud voice, even when new technology made this expenditure of energy unnecessary.

49

Whenever the speaker happened to pause for a moment, a shrill screech of shawms came toward us from far off. I heard them for the first, but not the last time, and even though I was surrounded daily by great music, the blaring and shrieking of this instrument—which couldn't be properly played, since it lacked half-notes—invariably stirred up in me a shuddering of fear and hope. In its undisguised ugliness, suffering and want became audible, along with the unarticulated urge toward dignity and beauty, which ought to exist for all. The shawms struck up the tune of "Brüder, zur Sonne." Bach and Mozart, no matter what they might have intended, had designed their monumental works for these masses wrapped in fog, but the shrill dissonance of the sound revealed what the stanza meant:

Look, how the columns of millions
Flow endlessly from the night
'Til the yearning of your desire
Swells over heaven and night.

Only a little more than two years had passed since this rally when I was standing near the Brandenburg Gate one evening. Around noon the Reich president had called on Hitler to head the government. A few hours later I tried to distribute leaflets in front of the Askania Works with a friend; they called for a general strike, although the unions had already refused. There were still no police in sight, yet many of the workers passing by no longer wanted to take a leaflet. Some took one, read the heading, and threw it away. "Too late, my boy," one man said. Rumors raced through the city. The night that was now falling would be the Night of the Long Knives announced long before. At this point we did not know that many such nights would follow. Late that afternoon I moved. A woman friend who lived in a garret gave me refuge. Through the open skylight I examined the roofs that would make escape possible in an emergency. But now I saw the torchbearers passing by. Snatched from the frosty darkness for a few seconds by histrionic spotlights, columns of SA, SS, and Stahlhelm, and more SA, SS, and Stahlhelm, singing incessantly, alternating the *Deutschlandlied* and the *Horst Wessel Lied*, other songs as well, a violent, blindly vindictive wind came out of the void, twisting like spark-spewing smoke above the half-crazed masses in the darkness, we had been taught these songs in the schools of the Republic.

> . . . that our old strength be put to the test
> whenever battle cries roar at us —
> Persevere in raging storm . . .

The columns marched down Wilhelmstrasse, where behind the lighted windows a senile old man was clumsily tapping the beat, while next to him the savior in proper frock coat raised his arm in salute. There was breathing, gasping, and bellowing all around me. The crowds that surged there, screaming and singing, were not intoxicated from the sort of alcohol that's served in taverns. Nearby, two well-dressed men, who obviously did not know each other, fell into an embrace. In the light of the torches I saw their large faces streaming with tears. "Germany is free!" stammered the one, and the other repeated, "Germany is free!" Monotonously and stubbornly a voice within me said: I'm not one of you, I don't want to be one of you. Behind the rumbling darkness I sensed the quiet forbearance of the country; silently I sensed the unconquerable melancholy of its music, the inaudible verses of its poets, its oracles and prophecies, its long, confused history, the mysterious introversion of its landscapes, the simple bravery of my friends. I was alone, and the angels of the fatherland stood all around me.

At that time when a slanting light shone on El Gesira and feasting on doves I gazed at the ruby-inlaid daggers in the belts of the celebrating sheiks when the fine unending rain fell on the hedges in Marienbad and on my brother and me when I was driving in a dead area and saw the impact from the machine-gun fire running along the road in front of the right front wheel when I lay wrapped in blankets beside the megalithic graves and the seal hunters were shooting out near the coast when Casals played the Schumann concerto in a hall full of wounded men when I stared at the heavyweight champion Giuseppe Spalla on the night train to Zurich and he stroked me on the head when on the road to Corbera I met the wounded man whose lower jaw was missing when we stopped in front of the small palace next to the French embassy and Max Liebermann took us up and showed us the sketches of Menzel and Degas when I said "Good morning" and the official silently pointed with his pencil to the sign "The German salute is used here" when I entered the port of Larnaka when Stravinsky was conducting The Firebird and I asked loudly why the Philharmonic was playing off-key when I got to know the beautiful strawberry blonde H. from Nuremberg in the coach of the Garde Mobile and I stood at night next to her bier which was shoved onto the train to Drancy because she was not yet dead when I was told my violin had a soul and I didn't know that referred to a wooden peg when S. walked with me across the Kremlin courtyard with his face downcast and without moving his head rolled his eyes upward and said "Up there is where *he* lives" when I rode late one afternoon on the streetcar from Limoges through the fields to Oradour-sur-Glane and the sun on the windows of the bakery blinded me and all the people were still walking around as usual when I always dreamed the same dream in which the glass doors between the rooms slid apart with a soft distant thundering and revealed a faceless white figure before whom I fell speechless and breathless to my knees when I was called Neubert when . . .

A new obscurantism awoke amid alarming news, vague fears, appeasing speeches. Sects arose overnight, spread, and displayed their colorful weekly papers on the walls of kiosks. The horoscope began to govern the lives of millions. The leader of the most influential of these sects was able to fill the Berlin Sportpalast whenever he convened a rally. He communicated with the spirits of Frederick the Great and Bismarck; they reported through their earthly medium that the future belonged to the nationalist forces. This sect's newspaper was distinguished by its particularly fantastic, eye-catching headlines. One morning in the last or next to last summer before the catastrophe I read one of these headlines: England will sink into the sea on August 19. The accompanying article explained that the Lord God would no longer tolerate the sins amassed by the British plutocrats, most of which had been committed against Germany; He had decided to let the island sink beneath the waves. The grim seriousness of the prediction seemed amusing, but my smile would soon vanish.

I waited with some impatience for the designated day and the edition of the newspaper following it. As the feeling of an inevitable defeat spread within me, I read the terse report that England had sunk into the sea on the date indicated. I knew it would be hopeless to try to convince the believers otherwise. Even if I pointed out that all the other papers, untouched by this news, would continue to bring the latest reports from England, even the evidence of English newspapers with stories about the royal family and the latest results of the tournament at Wimbledon, or an invitation to go to England together to convince ourselves with our own eyes of the island's continued existence — all this would be brushed off with the silent smile of superiority. For those who had decided to follow the master from now on and thus to live in the truth, every counterproof, every contradictory newspaper account, even the landing of a ferry in Folkestone or Dover, would be seen as deception and the work of the Devil. Precisely the opposition of others, their far superior numbers, and the power of their arguments would more firmly reinforce the blinded in their opinion — for there is a blind pride of the few, for whom the guarantee that they alone are in possession of salvation seems to lie precisely in their own insignificance and lack of persuasive power. Incapable of accepting any other reality, they would live from now on in a self-chosen one. Appalled, I anticipated the breakup of the previously familiar world into a multitude of chimerical realities, each of which would derive its own justification from itself, and among which no common denominator, no dialogue could exist.

One revelation of that time was the *Greuel-märchen*, the supposedly fictitious atrocity story; the minister of propaganda was the first to use the term; it made a stronger impression than those pallid, worn-out words "lies" and "slander." The new term designated the unauthorized dissemination of a public secret. It was forbidden to disclose facts outside the limited circle for which they were reserved. So we soon saw people being tortured for spreading the lie that torture existed in Germany.

I got accustomed to living among madmen. My whole life long I have been able to observe how madness spread and how it took hold in other countries. This was the only way possible to explain how thousands could still maintain, decades after the war, that they had known nothing about fascist atrocities. One who is emphatically talked into believing that what he sees does not exist, because if he held it to be the truth he would come to bodily or mortal harm, has to make a choice between death and madness.

After the war I ran into a friend from my youth; I had not seen her for fifteen years. We spent an afternoon and evening in conversation. People didn't know anything, she told me, they didn't suspect anything, if only she'd had an inkling of the crimes she had heard about after the war... I reminded her of my friend H. who was held captive for two weeks in a cellar by the SA and then had sought refuge with me. She had been there in my room when H. took off his shirt to show us his back, blackened by beatings. I still recall how her face changed after I reminded her of this scene. The look in her beautiful eyes, which had once enthralled me, now resembled that of someone half asleep who is only gradually awakening. I heard her faltering voice, as if from far away: "But of course... You're right... I remember..." Pity and horror wrestled within me; I took my leave.

In the summer or fall of 1933 I was sitting in a Berlin café watching a group of elegant young people at the next table, laughing and making malicious remarks as they took turns looking at an illustrated newspaper. I too had the *Berliner Illustrierte* in front of me. The latest edition of this paper, with a circulation of millions, featured a report several pages long on the concentration camp at Oranienburg. I saw a picture of prisoners pulling a road roller. I saw both the burning and extinguished eyes of unknown comrades and friends, who, as the accompanying text proclaimed, were to be won over to the "national community" through hard work and discipline. "We treat this riffraff much too decently," someone at the next table said. Many years later I asked myself how many millions had read this article and to how many more they had passed on what they had read. The young people next to me they were exchanging opinions about the Jewish-Bolshevik rabble, about the shaven heads, the burnt-out faces. Someone made a witty remark; diabolical laughter followed. *"Di rider finirai pria dell' aurora,"* sang the statue of the commendatore.

Whenever anyone bent over to ask him what he wanted to be, he always answered with unflappable seriousness that he wanted to be a pilot. The grownups would break into cries of disbelief and admonition; to be a pilot in those days was something totally out of the ordinary. My father chuckled with satisfaction. Flying meant something to him; even before the First World War he had flown. "If you really want to, Fredy, you'll be a pilot," he said. Some of his friends reproached him for endorsing the dangerous wish of a young boy rather than talking him out of it. During the long weeks my brother and I spent with our governess on the Baltic coast, a seaplane coming from inland sometimes roared directly over us. The people on the beach raised their heads, the plane touched down right off the coast, turned toward the beach, and stopped near us. My father jumped out wearing high boots; we greeted him wildly. He played an hour or two with us on the beach and then flew back to one of the lakes in Berlin. Fredy did not want to play long. He sat down in the wet sand right near where the last feeble waves died out; he looked seriously and intently at the plane as it rocked on the water. That's how he looked at everything he encountered, at a leaf, a bug, a snail in his hand. His gaze was never fleeting or distracted.

He was two years younger and much smaller than I; he had the greatest charm and was infinitely devoted to me. He had thought up an endearingly diminutive nickname for me and treated me as if I were the younger, more vulnerable one. He went along with everything I wanted: he played whatever games interested me at the time, he left the room when he was bothering me and I didn't want to see him. To share in my interests, he often asked about a book or piece of music, but I turned him away disdainfully. I was at the age when children show their first signs of cruelty. A few times I hit him when no one was around; once I even drew blood—he would fend me off hesitantly and cautiously as if he did not want to hurt me. Only once did he contradict me. We had several goldfish, and I suggested we cut them up to see what they looked like inside. "You mustn't do that," he said and looked at me seriously, "they're alive." He grew faster than I did and became strong and agile; we both went in for sports. After I had made some progress on the violin, my father arranged for him to take cello lessons, but it didn't work out, even though he had a good ear and the teacher thought he had talent. He gradually let it drop, and when he stopped altogether one day, no one seemed to notice.

The school he attended was evidently not right for him either. He left it and went to technical schools in Germany and England. Our relationship improved, he eagerly read the books I recommended to him, he went to concerts, he was the first one to learn the secret that I had become a Communist, for which he praised me wholeheartedly. "They're the only people you can really trust," he said, returning the copy of *State and Revolution* I had lent him. Technical things fascinated him, but he was the first person to whom I showed the poems I had begun writing. He had always been a brave boy; gradually something daredevilish, which filled me with a vague fear, came out in his personality. He began to ride motorcycles, bought himself a heavy Norton, and raced at eighty miles an hour over English country roads. "It's not what I really want," he said. "I'm still going to fly."

In the meantime he had begun to take flying lessons. We were young men by this time, he was half a head taller than I. For him I was still the brother he had to look out for, the one who would not get along so easily in life. He was handsome, serious yet affable, popular with everyone. He caught women's eyes. For some reason or other an acquaintance called him "high-spirited." Once we met with friends, we were lying on the beach and began wrestling playfully with one another. He was now much stronger than I and defeated me after a few minutes. When we got up, he laughed cheerfully and affectionately. There was no vanity in that laugh. He was not thinking back on the childhood days I had sometimes made difficult for him; he was happy because he had one more reason to defend and protect me.

When the war broke out, he succeeded in joining the RAF. It was difficult because he was born in Germany, but two members of the House of Commons vouched for him, and he flew bombers assembled in Canada over to England. But he did not like that either, he wanted to be a fighter pilot, and he became one. I was soon a captive in a captive land and did not hear anything from him until six months later when a message secretly reached me. He wanted me to describe exactly my daily routine and all the details of the area where I was then living. I suspected what he had in mind and had to smile when I thought about his illusions. Now and then people of political or military importance, people close to the general, were rescued from the occupied country and taken out by air. I was of no importance, I was a German emigrant, one of many.

Nevertheless I did what he requested of me; it was a game. I drew a small map and wrote out a routine in which I indicated the times of day when I knew precisely where I would be. He replied that he was in the process of putting the plan into action. A few weeks later he informed me that headquarters had rejected his request but that he would try again after a while, and he closed with his usual phrase of encouragement: "Keep your chin up!" His obvious disappointment amused me — what had he been thinking . . . Then I heard nothing more from him, ever again. Only after the war did I find out he had died in action early in 1943.

I received some information about him, a few notes he had made, as well as his last letter to me, which he had not sent, perhaps because the connection through which we passed messages back and forth no longer existed. The members of his squadron had liked him a lot, he was a good pilot and pursued the enemy with a vengeance, they had called him "Starlet." The terse diary entries I got to read disclosed hardly anything except a despairing longing for Germany, the kind one should not talk about to the Germans one normally meets, because it is incomprehensible to them. It is the feeling of those cast off, forced out, or exiled, of the cosmopolitans, as they are sometimes called. The letter I mentioned relates the dream of a young man who had gone to war in the hope that it would be the last. It describes how the dreamer finds himself in an endless space among the dead of all nations, their numbers increase steadily, they murmur in a mysterious language, "and," so the letter ends, "I realized that I had died in vain."

Sometimes I do not think of him for a long time. If I wake up at night and cannot fall asleep again, and if the sound of a lonely plane can be heard somewhere in the silent darkness, I can feel him approaching. Again I look over the gently undulating fields and meadows, while beyond the woods of St. Pierre-de-Fursac roars the thunder of a low-flying Spitfire. The time has nearly come, he will call me by the name he gave me when he was a little boy; he will take me to another country where there is no hate or fear, to a country that does not exist, a country near the sun, my high-spirited, my only friend.

I entered the hall behind the Palais Bourbon. The earth continued to tremble, the shooting in Spain had died down, after the Sudetenland it had been Prague's turn, Memelland and Albania were occupied, I had already seen how bombs fall, how oaths go up in smoke, how alliances are broken, I kept my eyes fixed on my friends; we were in the most difficult of struggles: to block the path of war. Statesmen made speeches in which one had to search for the sentence or dependent clause containing the dark, vaguely hinted threat. It was easy to lose heart; I already saw many people around me who were discouraged, cynical, or despondent. I did not despair, I could not, I always heard within me Luther's "We shall prevail." It remained that way. I was sustained by the feeling of belonging to a vanguard that showed humanity the only possible way, and even if I often quoted Rosa Luxemburg's *Socialism or Barbarism*, the alternative remained incredible and incomprehensible to me. I pushed the threatening "or" aside; just to mention the great goal seemed to reduce what I feared to insubstantial proportions.

I entered the hall in the fine fever of confidence that we were holding a conference against war and fascism, the last one, we still had two or three months left, all the languages of Europe buzzed around me, it seemed as if every smile were turned toward me with kindness, sympathy, and trust, perhaps because I was so young, I was one of the youngest delegates. I saw Paul Nizan with clouded brow leaning on the directors' table, I saw Andersen-Nexö, I saw Aragon, to whom I brought information about the Spanish refugees every few days to the Rue 4 Septembre. Clouds floated through the hall, a stormy joy entered me and filled me, I looked for my friends' table, a sign with the inscription "Allemagne" stood in the middle of the round table, I saw the faces of people I knew, Rudolf Leonhard, Franz Dahlem, Siegfried Rädel motioned to me, Heinrich Mann pointed to the empty chair next to his, he called me "young man," my joy and embarrassment kept me silent, How many of the dead had assembled around me, and why is Reichstag deputy Rädel carrying his head under his arm...

At that time the city was under a spell of endless celebration and a tense anticipation of great changes that would not subside. The old Prussian sound of fife and drums was heard continually from somewhere; small and large units of uniformed soldiers with standard-bearers in front passed tirelessly through the streets; the passers-by gathered to salute the flags in Roman fashion. Most did it cheerfully. Woe to him who failed to salute. Harangues and carefully articulated speeches echoed from loudspeakers. Every third day an occasion arose to drape the houses with flags; many people left the banners hanging from their windows all the time, and there were gradually more and more. Never before were so many cornerstones laid, so many new bridges and streets dedicated.

But there was not only celebration. Work was doggedly and furiously proceeding in a city of work, a city in which a third of the population had not been employed for years. Say what you will, the others were only windbags full of empty promises, but this one will do something—you'd hear people say this all over. Do something, yes, some argued, but to what purpose? Banners in Gothic letters spanned the streets, assuring people that anyone who had personally experienced war wanted nothing but peace. Already the first representatives of veterans' organizations were arriving from Paris and London to find this new Germany's love of peace confirmed. Those who believed they saw the roots of a new war in all that was happening were in the minority; they became fewer when the new regime's first open challenges of the other powers drew nothing but a feeble protest. These challenges were backed up by demonstrations of growing military might. Wasn't it clear (so went the triumphant response to doubters and admonishers) that this new army was not intended to be an instrument of war, but merely a means of political pressure, and that in restructuring European relationships, which would be inconceivable without German hegemony, the new army, by its threatening invincibility, would discourage any thought of armed resistance and thereby truly guarantee peace. Never before had teachers cited their "Si vis pacem" so often. Against this background, Lenin's admonition to search for the secret of war took on a strange, momentous ring. His warning began to reach far into the future. War would never tire of disguising itself as peace.

That spring a stream of foreigners flowed into the transformed country. People had heard so much about the dramatic changes; they had always feared but also marveled at Germany's violent energy. My cousin Geoffrey, a correspondent for a London newspaper, came to Berlin. He was four or five years older than I; I had met him once in England as a child, and he had hardly paid any attention to me. I lived on Steinplatz, and all one afternoon I took a walk with him between the Tiergarten and Tauentzienstrasse. Now and then we would sit down for a while at a café, lazily enjoying the warmth of spring and watching the cheerful, well-dressed people around us. No one in this part of town paid any attention to people not speaking German. I let Geoffrey talk, he must have had the impression I was an attentive listener, but only occasionally was I able to follow exactly what he said; once again a feeling of forlornness came over me, I was alone if my friends, my comrades-in-arms, were not with me, no one but us knew what was really happening, nobody else knew the truth. Somewhere right in the vicinity steel rods were whipping someone's back, cellar walls smothered the screams of the tortured. A rumor was going around that Prince August Wilhelm, a son of the Kaiser and a high-ranking SA leader, was practicing his villainy not far from here. Outside the city, and other cities as well, surrounded by heath and woods, were the first camps. Thousands had already perished in the cellars and camps, but no one noticed either the dead or the imprisoned. Millions of others were alive and would never be sent to a camp; they worked, went to the movies, sunned themselves on the beach at Wannsee, eyed the women, went to theaters and concerts, read the results of the last races at Mariendorf and Hoppegarten.

The day was just as beautiful as all the beautiful days there had ever been. Somewhere little girls were playing the ancient game of hopscotch. The most frightening thing was that nothing had changed, that life went on as merrily as always, while actually everything, right down to the children's games, should have been different. I knew exactly what would be in store for me, if I now got up and went out to Grunewald—already I thought I could feel the mild breeze and smell the sap of the pines; I was surrounded by the changeless indifference of nature. It would endure, always the same; only we would become different, no longer be able to live, no longer be allowed to live. Even now I was not the person I made myself out to be. I was seemingly a passerby, a customer at a café, one of many. I chatted, I appeared to be enjoying the day, but I was really an outcast, an enemy of this system, a person who disguised himself and did not reveal himself to this relative sitting across the table.

One had to admit, said Geoffrey, that even if one could talk about unpleasant conditions, England was not free of responsibility for them: after all, the Entente had acted narrow-mindedly and vindictively toward Germany. One shouldn't be surprised if a great people finally loses its patience.

Germany, I countered, lost its patience right at the moment when a timid republic, or what was still left of it, had overcome the worst consequences of Versailles after a great effort. Now we were busy preparing something for the others that would outdo Versailles.

It hasn't gone that far, said Geoffrey. Everything now depends on the understanding shown by the former Entente toward this new Germany. Real agreement would develop from such understanding.

"At our expense," I said, "and at the expense of eastern Europe."

Poland and Czechoslovakia were under the protection of France, my cousin replied. Anyway, one shouldn't get upset with an old and cultured people endowed with diligence, love of order, and ingenuity when it takes long-neglected, almost unpopulated regions under its protection: that could only be of benefit to everyone. Still, he would concede, he said, that a nation's concerted efforts to eliminate material suffering and unemployment using bold new methods, and to simultaneously overcome a certain discrimination, must in some respects lead to unpleasant consequences as well. Of course, these are internal affairs in which other nations should not get involved. One thing, in any case, must be emphasized: a canon of civilized behavior, as important as it may be for human coexistence, could not be valid everywhere at all times. Revolutions have their own laws; one must permit them a certain right to excesses and give them time to overcome childhood illnesses. "Certainly some leaders here have bad manners," Geoffrey said, "but if we show ourselves to be understanding, in time they will discard them."

I said nothing. I saw how he scrutinized those sitting around us and the passersby with a look combining watchfulness, respect, and a certain distaste. Visitors at the zoo sometimes assume this expression as they stand in front of the cages of predators.

Incidentally, Geoffrey added, people abroad are quite displeased with the way the new state is treating the Jews. This was truly deplorable.

"If you were German," I said, "you would be considered to be of Jewish descent. You'd better not go too far with your criticism. Remember that objectivity is called for."

He was silent for a moment. His face showed that he was irritated and insulted. Well, he replied, even if I was ironically demanding objectivity from him, I could hardly deny that the Jews had lacked tact and restraint at times, that they — certainly not all of them, but not so few either — had occasionally been too aggressive and rubbed some people the wrong way.

If one had practiced restraint out of necessity, I said, always between one pogrom and the next, and this over an endless period of time, one might naturally be tempted in later, more emancipated times to relax this peculiar self-discipline. When one is told he has equal rights, he eventually begins to believe it. However, it soon became obvious, I said, that in order to be taken seriously at all a person had to accomplish something exceptional. Of course, one could define *Das Kapital* or psychoanalysis or *Remembrance of Things Past* as a kind of pushiness, not to mention music or the natural sciences, but this splendid definition perhaps permitted conclusions to be made about the person making it and about his concept of equal rights.

Unfortunately, Geoffrey said, barbarism plays its role in history when it is a matter of getting the stagnating blood of old civilizations to flow faster again.

I thought of the famous poet who had encouraged my poetic attempts a few years before and now shouted good riddance after my emigré friends, that history was mutating and a people wanted to ennoble itself. "The faster flowing blood of old civilizations," I said, "is something very real: it flows from young workers they dragged to the scaffold." Geoffrey and I stood up at the same time. I could tell that he had finally had enough of me.

The first of May had been proclaimed a national holiday; it was now called "Labor Day." I saw the workers of Berlin moving toward the Tempelhof Field by the hundreds of thousands. Their parties were disbanded, their elected leaders incarcerated or dead or on the run, their union buildings plundered and occupied. Standing on the curb, I saw them pass by; they were now called "the workforce" and the employers at the front "operation leaders." The new names corresponded to old Germanic social categories, it was claimed, and all those who passed by were called the national community, the *Volksgemeinschaft*, because the new government had proclaimed that there were no classes any longer. It was against Jewish Marxism and greedy capitalism, but for the productive German entrepreneurs Krupp and Röchling.

The workers marched under a bright but hardly warming May sun, and around them rose a vision of ancient Rome. I thought I saw the generals we had been reading about in school, as they paraded conquered peoples through their capital. The workers looked as they always had; only a discerning eye perceived barely noticeable changes in them: their clothes, their gestures, their attitude. As always they were poorly fed and wore clean, threadbare suits and those seaman's caps that served in those days as a universal outward sign of their class. The caps were trimmed with an unobtrusive band, most often of black patent leather, which many replaced with a leather band and a buckle. Social Democrats and Communists wore this kind of band on their caps, the National Socialists another kind that was divided in the middle.

It was this minute difference that suddenly caught one's eye, and the banal fact that more people than ever before wore the divided band on their caps communicated the fateful news of a lost battle and what usually follows: shame, lethargy, and compulsory or affected adaptation. In the pockets of the defeated were the newspapers of the regime; in them they could find not only the insults and the triumphant derision of the victors, but also the veiled invitation to treason under the guise of sympathy: "Your leaders have brought you to this point. They themselves are sitting safely in Paris and Moscow." The awareness of being abused and lied to was mixed with the consciousness of being powerless and without a voice; a stench of decay hovered over the city as it roared with loudspeakers and brass bands. With dread I sensed this decay in myself for a moment: like an aurora borealis of disintegration, the wish surged up in me to be among the marchers, to let myself be carried along with them, to be driven by the same power that controlled them. Something in me opposed the tempter. Already the mouths of those moving by, who just a few months ago had sung the old Spartacus song, shaped new words to the familiar melody. Might not the present rulers be right, since they had been victorious . . .

Although the people we had been talking about betrayed their mission, it cannot be forgotten that they, the majority, were also the weakest, the most oppressed, and the most dependent. They, who were not occupied with living but with the reproduction of their manpower, sinned against themselves when they were not prepared, when they were not capable of uniting. They paid for their self-righteousness, their defiance, and their arrogance with tens of thousands of slain and tortured, as well as with the humiliation of no longer being allowed to call themselves proletarians.

But the submission encompassed much more, it encompassed all segments of the population, the parties not yet banned, the churches, the newspapers, the clubs, the universities, the courts, the publishing houses. Every day it became more naked, more shameless, more obtrusive. The submission had a thousand faces; not only the defectors became visible, who again broke up into various categories, for to the more straightforward sort it was like scales falling from their eyes, while others, who had been known as members of a democratic party, pulled a second party membership book out of their pockets, which proved them to be long-time, loyal fighters for the victorious revolution. There were also those who hung up their convictions, which had long been on display, on a nail as they would hang up a summer suit for the winter; they too became visible, and in doing so they would let you know with an assuring wink that they could be counted on when the time came.

We heard speeches and read articles that we would not have believed the speakers and writers capable of a few days earlier: they had been considered leftists. Those who had not yet mastered fascist jargon, or in whom some vestiges of shame still remained, tried to make it clear, at least through the use of some concept or cliché, that they understood and affirmed the deeper significance of what was happening, though with certain reservations. They were always able to inject phrases at certain points that sounded like "consciousness of our national values," "National Revolution," "long-awaited emergence of the people," or simply "blood." This took place in the days and weeks before ideological conformity, the *Gleichschaltung*, was decreed.

Of my schoolmates, among whom I hardly had a friend because we had all become too deeply divided by conflicting points of view, I saw only a few after our final examinations and then mostly by chance.

I liked Götz von R., the son of an army general. He was smaller than I, had a round, happy face, and liked to make fun of the National Socialists. He did not ridicule the Communists; he took them seriously, labeled himself their opponent, but was interested in Marxist theory and especially in the Soviet Union, which his father knew well— he was one of those high-ranking officers who had been in contact with the Red Army. Götz von R. considered a German pact with Russia essential to survival, regardless of the regime in power there. Before Hitler's takeover, I gave him the *Aufbruch* to read; it was published by former officers and right-wing activists who had become Communists. Among the editors were Beppo Römer, the former Freikorps leader, and the writers Ludwig Renn and Bodo Uhse, people I eventually came to know personally. Circumstances made me soon lose track of Götz von R. The last time we were together he offered to hide me in his parents' house, if I happened to be in danger. I laughed and thanked him. The year before the war ended I heard his name one night over London radio: the American navy had sunk a German U-boat that day; the skipper, Lieutenant Commander Götz von R., had been taken prisoner.

I had a peculiar relationship with B. He was the son of an officer killed in the First World War. His poverty-stricken mother had made great sacrifices so that he could attend school and receive musical training. He became a member of the Hitler Youth and the SA at the same time that I joined the Communist Youth Organization, the only student in my school to do so. B. hated Marxists, Jews, and foreigners. As a pupil of Wilhelm Kempff, he also played the piano splendidly. We once came to blows briefly, but because I knew how to box and put him in his place, he never acted belligerently toward me after that. He was one of those many cringing characters who only build up courage and become dangerous in a pack. It would not be long before this pack would be ruling Germany and singing "When the Jew's blood spurts from the knife, then we'll be twice as well-off." But things had not gone so far yet, and we discussed musical matters earnestly and often.

In the spring of 1935 we met repeatedly for several evenings, when Claudio Arrau played the entire works of Bach for piano. Arrau, who had played publicly with my teacher several times, was one of the very few foreign musicians who could still be heard in Germany at that time. During the intermissions I chatted with B. The prevailing conditions would have made it possible for him to finally take his revenge on me. But he had not changed his behavior since the time we had gone our separate ways after our final examinations. We discussed whether it was appropriate to play certain figurations legato. As we did so, I saw the troubled, hate-filled look directed at me from his small slanted eyes. For the first time I thought about the real or apparent truce which great works of art are able to establish between stubborn opponents or enemies who are equally versed in art. Later on I encountered this phenomenon several more times but could not rid myself of the suspicion that a misunderstanding must have existed on at least one of the two sides.

In the jargon of the day G. was also what was called an old warrior. He was intelligent and, unlike B., entirely without malice — much more friendly, and straightforward by nature. There was something visionary about him. He was not in good health and had some mysterious disability: every few days or weeks his face would turn terribly pale right in the middle of class. He became stiff and unresponsive and would sink over to one side where the person next to him would support and hold him up. The lesson was interrupted when this happened, and we would look anxiously at G., who would recover after two or three minutes and take part in the lesson again as if nothing had happened. This vulnerable but good-natured young man, who was interested in intellectual matters, was not actually what one would imagine an SA man to be, yet he was one. We were not friends, we could not be; but we felt a certain affinity for one another. Sometimes we joked about whether we might have fired shots at each other one of the last few nights, for during those brief skirmishes in the streets at night we would first shoot out the streetlights so as not to give the opponent a clear target — we couldn't be seen, and could see only shadows in the dark.

I met G. on Wittenbergplatz one night shortly before I left Germany. We walked for a while; he began talking about politics and after a few minutes asked me point-blank: "Are you still a Communist?" I hesitated, but an outlaw quickly develops an instinct for how far he can go with someone. I replied that he, G., knew me well and so he must know that I did not change philosophies the way a person changes shirts. He showed no surprise, nodded a couple of times, and said: "I thought as much. But I've changed." It was up to me to be surprised. "Aren't you a National Socialist any longer?" I asked. "Of course," he said quietly, "but we will have to form a new movement. Adolf Hitler has betrayed us. A social revolution has not taken place." He was one of those who had believed staunchly in the revolutionary nature of this counterrevolution and now was one of the few who was ready to draw conclusions from his disappointment. We shook hands. I never saw him again either.

The wave of history broke over my schoolmates, and it also snatched my friends into nothingness. Fritz K. was a messenger boy for a medium-sized company in Berlin; small, blond, wiry, endearingly impudent, he was always ready with a joke. I had tried in vain to interest him in books and pointed to our friend Heinrich as an example. Heinrich was an avid, incessant reader — first Shakespeare, then Darwin. He looked upon me as the owner of a lending library, a role I assumed with delight. But Fritz didn't stay with books very long. One couldn't blame him, for he'd always have another joke up his sleeve, he preferred going to meetings and demonstrations; he was cheerful, courageous, and loyal, a Berlin *gavroche*. He fell as one of the first victims of the war outside the gates of Warsaw.

I was very fond of Walter N. He was a mason by trade, strong and imposing, more inclined to thinking and reflecting than to speaking, since he suffered from a speech impediment. A few days after Hitler seized power I went to see him in the hope of winning him over to the underground. He refused. He explained to me that the Labor Front had offered him a place in a training program free of charge; when he completed it, he would be able to take the exam for foreman. "You can certainly understand that I have to take advantage of this opportunity. I've also just gotten a job for the first time in three years. And after I'm a foreman, I can do a lot more for the cause. And we're all in favor of people being qualified..." Walter N. marched east with millions of others; he wound up in a Soviet prison camp and was released shortly after the war. Everything would have turned out well, but he took a drink of water from the tender on the train bringing him home. By the time the train crossed the border he already had typhus, and he died in less than three days.

Albert H., who came from my home town, fought in Spain. While advancing over a section of captured terrain, he noticed a wounded Franco officer acting as if he wanted to surrender. When Albert went up to him, the officer drew his pistol and shot him in the groin at close range. Albert shot and killed the fascist, then they rushed him off. Like many of the seriously wounded in the brigades, he was taken to the Soviet Union. The wound healed, but he had ceased to be a man. When the attack on the Soviet Union began, he volunteered for a parachute mission over Germany. He and others remained missing in action. Only after the war were his files and the brief entry about his death found with the Gestapo. The attached photograph was the only evidence that this was Albert H. Despite being tortured, he had given away no information, not even his name. He had been executed as "unknown."

L ate one winter evening during my second year with the underground, frozen stiff after coming back by bicycle from a conspiratorial meeting, I was listening to Radio Moscow in my little room and found out there had been an assassination that day in Leningrad. Sergei Kirov, the secretary of the Leningrad party organization, had been shot dead. Kirov's name was hardly known outside the Soviet Union. I had seen it once or twice; a picture revealed a still youthful lion's head with an energetic mien. The assassin, it was reported, had been arrested, and his co-conspirators were being sought.

I had already gotten used to asking the question "Who would benefit by this?" A justified and necessary question, to be sure, but one which can be answered all too often in an abbreviated, voluntaristic sense, and which also instantly gives the impression that the questioner is in possession of far-reaching certainties. That the archenemies of communism, the National Socialists, had to be interested in the assassination as part of a plan of total destruction was quite clear to me, even before I heard it from commentaries that were not long in coming. In the next few days there were reports that the conspirators had been arrested. There were old revolutionaries among them — Zinoviev, Kamenev, and others. The mention of these names caused me the greatest consternation. But was it not a fact that every revolution had produced traitors? Were not one-time leaders of revolutions often enough embroiled in treason, and to such a degree that it was actually the appearance of these apostates that first confirmed the revolution as a fact?

These thoughts and the articles in the National Socialist newspapers, which reported the events in a tone of forced objectivity, though not without sarcasm, transformed my mourning for Kirov into a kind of grim satisfaction directed, as it were, against the enemy. In the quiet derision of these articles I thought I perceived a poorly suppressed rage over the revelation of wide-ranging plans. A leader of workers had fallen, but Stalin's eye was unerring; he would expose everyone who stood in our way.

I had plans to meet with E., whom I had not seen in a long time. I had received a message from him setting the time and place for our meeting. On the way I tried to remember when and where we had last seen each other, but I could not. The place was no longer fixed in my memory; it seemed to be infinitely long ago. It was almost dark when I arrived at the designated place, and I noticed with apprehension and astonishment that I was standing in the very garden of my childhood. The phosphorescent gravel on the narrow paths shone in the growing darkness, I saw the yew hedge standing like a shadow, the brightly painted furniture in the summerhouse stood out against the black background. Suddenly it occurred to me that E. had died in battle many years ago near Gandesa. I was alone, the darkness had become even more intense, I was afraid and called his name. But no one answered; it was as if one curtain after another swept down over the darkness that surrounded me, making it blacker and blacker.

During my childhood years I had never become familiar with the northern part of Berlin. I first got to know it cursorily during the three short years between the time the National Socialists came to power and my departure from Germany.

On a day in late summer I found myself on the Schönhauser Allee diagonally across from the large brewery, whose elongated building serves other purposes today. I was at the place where the tracks of the elevated train disappear underground. I had bought a bag of cherries at a store and had sat down on one of the three or four benches arranged in a semicircle there. The bench on my far right had been freshly painted yellow, the centuries-old color of disgrace. Shortly before, the Nuremberg Laws had been proclaimed. "For Jews only" was printed in black letters on the backrest of the yellow bench. There were quite a few poor Jews, mostly craftsmen and shopkeepers, living in this district. One of the city's old Jewish cemeteries was only a few yards away; a friend of my family, the painter Max Liebermann, had been laid to rest there a few months before.

I had not been sitting there very long when two huge men came toward me from across the boulevard. They were not simply big, they were gigantic, like the caryatids at the entrances of the houses built during the early years of the Empire. Their powerful bodies were covered by brass-studded leather aprons. I had seen men like them many times before. At that time beer kegs were still brought to stores and taverns by two- or four-team wagons; on the driver's seat of these imposing, festive wagons sat these brawny men, who drove the massive Oldenburg and Belgian horses. The animals, resembling their masters in power and dignity, were always beautifully adorned, their manes braided with ribbons, the brass studding on their harnesses flashing. The two blond, red-faced men ambled toward me, obviously intending to spend their morning break at this spot. They were carrying bottles of beer and packages of sandwiches for a mid-morning snack; they did not so much as glance at me. One of them was about to sit down on the bench next to me when the other put up his hand to stop him. "No, Karl," he said in a deep voice, which first had to work its way out of him and sounded like a quiet roar, "no, not here. Over there's our place." And both of them moved on and sat down on the bench bearing the inscription "For Jews only." With methodical movements they earnestly began their meal, without observing their surroundings, silent except for the occasional monosyllabic remarks that they growled back and forth with an impenetrable expression. I had to turn away.

In Lenin I had read that even the slightest trace of anti-Semitism is evidence of the reactionary character of the group or individual that exhibits it. I could see that this remark contained a kind of formula, a quasi-mathematical equation. Wherever the cowardly pestilence raised its head, there could be no socialism, all noble words to the contrary. Millions here willingly followed an insanity that called itself "national socialism."

I knew that I could not say anything to these two men. But I would never forget their hulking bodies, their exhaustion, their contempt for a miserable era, their silent nobility. Forsaken by their own kind, they defied the mob.

Toward evening I walked down the hill from the house and crossed a small wooded area, passing the gardener's house with its cooing doves. On the other side of the road was the dock, where I sat down to write some poetry. To my right I saw the bridge of Ferch, in front of me the Havel, turning pale in the evening, then becoming darker. In some places the setting sun enflamed the waters; through the abrupt spray of light swam small agile grebes. The near and distant calls of birds had a hesitant, weary sound.

I had been writing poems since I was eleven or twelve. Mostly they were inspired by other poems I liked, or an idea I found in them. I was interested in poetic forms and tried my hand at sonnets and eight-line stanzas. Right in the middle of my efforts, I would realize that what I was writing was no good. I felt that my thoughts were not worth communicating and furthermore that I was incapable of subordinating feeling and thought to the form I had chosen. From time to time I destroyed what I had accumulated, but my childish vanity could also not refrain from showing my parents and some of their acquaintances this or that poem. The praise I so desired, and which was abundantly bestowed upon me, made me feel ashamed as soon as I received it.

On that evening in Ferch I had nothing particular in mind, I had not been thinking of specific meters or stanzas. The evening grew deeper, the call of the birds faded. Motionless, I looked at the verses I had just completed. I did not know whether what I had written was really good, but I felt that it was my first poem. I was fifteen years old at the time.

I owe it to chance that I have the poem in my possession. It was published a year later in a small anthology that I found decades later, years after the war, in a second-hand bookstore. I have lost several other poems that were also published. It was precisely these poems I never showed to anyone except my brother.

On the dock in Ferch I experienced for the first time how a poem comes into being. I had had no plan, no goal, I had not thought of a rhyme scheme, evening fell, I sensed an imperceptible movement that must have already been there before I perceived it, gentle, but more emphatic than the lapping of the tiny waves against the pilings of the dock, a rhythmical ebb and flow in me and a breathing weariness like that of the darkening waters. Two or three disjointed words floated on this pulsating ground.

From this moment on I began to take my poems seriously, though not all too seriously; I was preserved from the latter by the gradually growing conviction that what had already been achieved in poetry and music, especially in Germany, could hardly be surpassed. But the statement of one poet, that a person might produce six worthwhile lines during his lifetime, made me think. Another poet contradicted this, by the way. Since I knew that he imagined each of his own words, with which he was not particularly thrifty, as being chiseled in marble from the start, his rebuttal hardly made an impression on me. The first poet's proposition seemed to me more important: it did not leave me entirely without hope.

Writing poems became a habit. They were there, it seemed, I had only to call them up when I needed them. What I produced was necessarily influenced by my personal life, by the political goals I wanted to achieve together with others, by the society that seemed to me to be worth striving for. Easiest of all was everything I wrote between the ages of twenty-two and thirty—the year the war ended; several months earlier my first collection of poetry had appeared in Zurich. I remember walking one day from bookstore to bookstore on the Bahnhofstrasse and being able to see my book in every window.

I was elated, as if I had finally delivered a message that had long been weighing on me. This naive satisfaction never again presented itself.

I was able to read many kind things about myself, but soon some misgivings were also heard. According to these critics, I was incorrigibly adept, despite all my talent, at formalistic and unnecessarily difficult methods. We were going through times which many people characterized by the commonplace expression "complicated." Following my own convictions, I made attempts to change. The desire to be useful dominated for a while. A woman friend from another country whom I told about this contradicted me vigorously: no poetry could be of any use in the way I suggested, least of all for the readership I envisioned. Poetry's real "benefit," provided that anyone wanted to use this absurd term, lay in its unmistakable ability to give new names to what is seemingly familiar, in its rejuvenating function, in its conjuring up what has been forgotten. As she went on speaking, I felt myself less and less able to follow what she was saying. I could not completely disagree with her, but I saw poetry, including my own, as inextricably bound by its historical context. I could not stand outside the time I lived in, and I too embraced impure, and not pure poetry. In the course of my life I had met poets of the second type in many countries, and some of them had become friends of mine.

As the sound of my friend's words became more and more faint, I saw poetry's long trail of blood reach from the days of Ch'ü Yüan and Ovid, through those of André Chénier and Hölderlin, and across the barren landscape of Harrar right up to our own day, it ran through exile, imprisonment, and death. I stood by the pit into which this blood flowed, before I too climbed down to the shadows. I also thought of the days when poetry had protected me from becoming callous and apathetic, when I carried three small volumes in my pocket, which I forced myself to read every day, through wars and beneath "wanted" posters. A Hölderlin, a Shelley, a Baudelaire, my entire library.

In the course of time, the verses I wrote gradually disappeared from my life. They vanished like a slight pain a person has already grown used to, until one morning, surprised and not without a feeling of emptiness, he wakes up to find it gone. Nobody bore responsibility for it except me. The voice that had once spoken fell silent, as so many conflicting voices began to speak in me. Sometimes, for no reason, there began that ebb and flow which

I had known since that evening on the dock at
Ferch, and which I observed sunken within myself.
I did not move, I merely felt how it came and went.

From time to time I visited my father. He had given up arguing with me about politics since our last heated debate, when I had refused to go to Cambridge. When he asked why, I had replied that the German revolution was at stake and that I wanted to stay with the workers. Sometimes I tried to persuade him to leave the country. He smiled and looked past me: "What for?" After a pause he added: "Germany is a prison, of course, but a comfortable prison... By the way," he went on, "it's been a long time since I've made as much money as I'm making now. You have to hand it to those gentlemen, they're doing a lot for the economy." He asked me whether I needed anything. I reassured him that I was managing all right with my earnings. His look indicated that he did not want to talk any more. He sat down at the piano, and we played Mozart sonatas.

He had always been a person who did not like to talk. He was friendly in a distant, absent way, so lost in his silence and dreams that it often took him a few long minutes to find his way back to reality when someone spoke to him persistently or asked him questions. Then an expression of growing anxiety came over his face, and since I had begun to fall into a similar state of mind as a young man, I needed no explanations for his behavior. "How much like him you really are," I began to hear at an early age. No matter how far life drew us apart, I always felt close to him. I did not need to ask what was going on inside him, because I was nothing more than the image of him. Perhaps he knew it; this thought consoles me after such a long period of mostly fragmentary talk, which ended in stony silence with his death decades ago.

Long before breakfast and before the arrival of his secretary, he would still play for two hours from the *Well-Tempered Clavier* as day was breaking. He played the piano as wonderfully as ever; he played more than ever during this time he endured with contempt. Music had always been what made life bearable for him, and now he spent a large part of his day with it. Sometimes he invited me to play with him; I was not a bad violinist but was not on a par with him. Nevertheless, he praised me because, as he expressed it, I understood what I was playing. Chamber music, which had been commonplace at our home in earlier years with an ever-changing group of musicians, was almost never played now—our friends and partners had left or preferred not to visit us any more.

Once my father and I saw a friend on one of the few walks we took together; he was one of Germany's most remarkable younger composers. He had been a frequent guest in our house over the years and was one of the numerous artists my father had helped. Now he hurried to get to the next cross-street, hastily turning the corner so that he would not have to greet us. He never came to our house again, as I later found out. He made no artistic concessions to National Socialism; his best work premiered during the war with one of the most famous ensembles of the Reich and was banned by the propaganda minister the following day. Many years later I met him again. He spoke with great feeling for my family and me; he asked about my father; I told him he had been taken to Sachsenhausen on the Crystal Night. Nothing actually unpleasant had ever come between us. From a certain moment on, he simply did not want to be associated with us. Only much later did I understand that the feeling of being obligated to someone is only acknowledged by people with inner strength; for the weak, however, a feeling of obligation is totally unbearable and even provokes them to aggression against those to whom they are indebted. This man was neither one of the truly strong nor one of the weak; he was one of that majority which makes up a third category. I often ran into him in the period that followed, it was unavoidable. We never mentioned the time he avoided us on the street or our losing touch with him. Sometimes a hounded, furtive look came over his face, as if he knew that I knew, that I remembered. This expression embarrassed me. I did not want to make him feel ashamed, but neither was it up to me to dispel his suspicions. Such encounters only strengthened me in my new feeling for life, which combined the desire to scream and total indifference. It expressed the kind of distress I had been through and at the same time something that sustained me, something that made it possible for me to continue to exist.

Of what befell my father later on I know only a little, from a few witnesses. One of my friends, a young metalworker, had seen him toward the end of the year, dressed in thin denim, breaking stones at Sachsenhausen. He knew, my friend said, that my father had never done physical labor before; he had also seen him carrying heavy loads without complaint after his committal to the camp, that had been particularly appalling. Right up to the end my father had maintained a peculiar attitude, combining discipline, politeness, and contempt, with regard to the SS.

Before all this happened, he had become more and more deeply isolated in the country that he did not want to abandon. He would either sit at the piano or pace back and forth among the pictures he had collected over many long years. At this time I was already living in other countries. When I think of him, I do not envision him as he was in his last years, which actually had not been years we spent together anyway. I see him as youthful, brisk, and elegant among elegant people. I myself stand beside my governess in the background, small, silent, and inconspicuous. Someone near us said to the person next to him: "What a lovely man!" I wondered: how could he be lovely, he was simply my father. We often had company at our house. If people arrived in the afternoon, they sometimes wanted to see my brother and me, and we would be led, both of us or just me, into the rooms where the guests were. They greeted us with friendly exclamations and soon forgot us. Once my father, who was chatting with some people, caught sight of me standing forlorn in a corner. He broke off his conversation, took me by the hand, and led me into another room, where he suddenly lifted me up, hugged me, and kissed me desperately without a word. It was a sweet and frightening moment; I fought for air under this devouring kiss, I struggled in his arms, for he had not shaved smoothly that day and his cheeks were scratching me. He put me down and took me to the playroom, and when I looked up at him, I was perplexed to see tears in his eyes for the first and last time.

But I see him immediately stepping back into the playroom, which actually seldom happened. It must have been a year or two later, I was about six years old. I should hold out my hands, he said, he had something for us to play with. He had two small metal objects, the medals he had brought back from the war. We didn't know what to do with them, but they lay for a long time among our stuffed animals and little wooden cars. Later I found out that my father, who had shared the wild nationalistic views of the great majority in 1914, had come back changed, transformed. Only very seldom did he forbid us anything, but my brother and I were forbidden to own toy soldiers, something we complained about bitterly and uncomprehendingly. He hit me only once. I was about thirteen, and during the course of a dinner conversation I no longer remember except that it obviously dealt with politics, I ventured the remark that we would make sure to regain our rights, and Alsace-Lorraine besides. My father turned red at these words, he got up without saying a word, walked over to my chair, and slapped me in the face. Then he left the room. Only later did it occur to me that he never mentioned the war, and that every time someone brought up the topic in conversation, he would sink into a long silence.

By the end, when he actually appeared to be waiting for the catastrophe, alone and lost in music, he had changed almost all his habits. He did not wait to be urged to resign from his club; he announced his resignation. He did not buy any more paintings, he sold a lot of them. I did not ask about them, I accepted the fact that I would miss this or that work during my infrequent visits; I could still look at the beautiful, eerie Odilon Redon with those flowers that do not bloom on earth but emerge from the smoke; the portrait of my parents by Corinth still hung in the large room. Long after the Second World War, when I had not thought about my father's pictures for a long time, I saw in the museum at Oslo a Munch which for years had hung over his desk. It depicted the silhouette of a man at the window of a darkened room as a glowing ship passes by on the dark sea. But not only were many paintings missing, my father had also sold the horses, for he did not ride any more. It would have been strange, in any case, if he had tried to retain this custom, now that the gentlemen from the Mounted SA were romping in the Tiergarten. I had not had a horse for a long time now; my father had been disappointed when he had noticed that I did not especially like to ride and actually only did it for his sake.

In earlier years, as a child, I had met him daily when I went walking with my governess. In dry weather I was allowed to take my little bicycle along, and I rode right next to the riding trail that ran parallel to the Charlottenburger Chaussee, up and down the small mounds of earth that had been piled up against the old trees in front of the façade of the Technical College. Already visible from afar through the rows of trees, he came toward us trotting English style, always riding alone. A light mist lit up by the invisible sun lay between the fall-colored trees as leaf after leaf floated down. Delighted, I watched him approaching, seated so casually and cheerfully on his horse. "Papa!" I called. But he did not answer. Without breaking gait, he rode on, glanced obliquely down at us or a little past us with his familiar smile, and merely raised the switch to the brim of his hat. We stood still and gazed after him, while behind us the tires of an occasional car hissed on the asphalt, and saw rider and horse fade in the golden mist.

*H*eran, *heran . . .* What is it beginning now, what can it be. You high heaven, you tender look. *Heran, heran.* For the last time. All of you, you and you and you, *heran, heran, was wiegen kann.* Do you remember, do all of you remember. Don't let it be heard, don't let it happen. Quieter still, quiet, let no one hear us, no one disturb us. In the deepest deep, we already knew it, come, it's time, says a voice, now we'll go to bed, be a nice boy, will you, the high glass door rolls shut, the voices recede, and once again the introductory theme, they are not yet satisfied with the first movement, how wonderfully the piano surges up, the music doesn't fit here, its wild, insatiable lament that tries vainly to hide behind a salon atmosphere, and why this paraphrase of a famous mazurka, and even the dedication "To the memory of a great musician" can't hide what it's really about, and holding N.'s hand I step into my room, there is my bed, a faithful light shines, *gute Ruh, gute Ruh! tu die Augen zu!* And the warm slow rain, falling from the smooth, motionless light-gray sky onto my half-closed eyelids as I lie half-hidden under the hedge by the road, before me the empty meadows, and ringing across them the faraway sounds of a village. The wind has died down, and my eyes look up to the motionless treetops above the dripping and murmuring of the waters, the rivulets, the brooks, the rivers. *Wandrer, du müder, du bist zu Haus.* Those are not the waters, there behind the door, it's you, it's all of you, is it possible, so near and I didn't know it, and now E.'s voice too, which my father accompanies, *woget und wieget den Knaben mir ein,* and now the pale, red-edged folds of carnations in the beds between the rows of pruned poplars, while the water flows over the horses that rear up out of the pool and race up to the fortress towering in the distance. Around its gray stone masses lie the evening clouds in a greenish and rosy sky. How fortunate that sleep was always nearby, one could flee to it, escape into it, even then, even there, even here, even now, you, the other one, longed for, closely distant, sky that now turns a darker hue, and always the changing clouds, the borders of the landscape receding, an undulation of volcanic hilltops with their forts, behind them lie the Pyrenees, the cathedral invisible somewhere to the north, the battles that long ago fell silent, shadows that wander across the hillsides, *daß ihn dein Schatten, dein Schatten nicht weckt.* But in the house tranquility reigned, the distant bells made it deeper, only the rustling of the pages of a book could be heard, a soft footstep in the hall, the green light of the chestnut trees still billowing outside the windows, the snow already falling unceasingly into my half-sleep, who was it singing softly beside me, what was the voice singing, what was it they sang by my cradle. Sweet sound of the blackbird, behind snowfall and foliage a time was formed that was always the new time, condemning and promising, always the threshold to an unseen future approaching finally and irrevocably, suddenly this new time stood all around me, I was in it, selected by fortune to take part in it, I had known nothing about it, suspected nothing, now it surrounded me, it was as if I had been waiting for nothing else, behind the forests of silence I had perceived its cataracts, now I darted along in the midst of its currents and shoals, I had not been able to choose it for myself, it was an Augustan era that bore me, behind it lay the gradually crumbling, decaying republics in their bygone austere beauty, before it the invasions of the barbarians, its empty, statuelike gaze disregarding the ruins it had amassed. A thousand voices encircled me, they screamed and breathed, they tempted and enticed, they promised and mocked, I listened and answered, it didn't matter whether anyone heard me, the sun had passed its zenith, painlessly age had come, I had risen from the shadow of the hedge, I still heard the song *Die Treu ist hier, sollst liegen bei mir,*

I would have to look at my watch to see whether it was time to get home in time, there is no watch, I must have forgotten it, it's lying somewhere in my room, and still the soft call *Heran, heran*. Night comes over the mountains. No, we don't want to part yet, let's just play the little Beethoven trio, not one of the big ones, the little one, Opus 11, we still have enough time for that, I'm lying down already, it's my bed, I have awakened and look up through the square window, the second movement begins with a rising fourth, followed by a rising fifth, a great look upward, the world could be good, you can bear your burden without turning pale, without screaming, *dîtes ces mots Ma Vie Et retenez vos larmes*, the night, the night, there is E.'s voice again, the gaze upward through the square window, *der Vollmond steigt, der Nebel weicht*, the night over the forests, over the sea, over the mountains, the silence that drowns out the empty noise, and the mighty, the incessant rocking, and the gaze upward that no longer turns away *und der Himmel da oben, wie ist er so weit*.

I dreamed I was crossing the tracks of the Vienna Railroad to the nearby station of the cable railway, which was right in the middle of the town and led from Sankt A. up to the northern mountain chain. I felt like a child, but I clearly saw the modern cars in the parking lot near the cable car and I was surprised that I had already been grown up a long time and was not even young any more. At the moment I bought my ticket at the window, a decision had matured inside me which seemed to be irrevocable, although I did not want to think about it. Already the cable car sailed off with me, it was jammed with vacationers in mountain-climbing garb, I too was wearing hiking boots, I quickly checked to make sure of that, then I looked out, the hotels and cars rapidly grew smaller, a window was open, I was holding a ring of keys in my hand and let it fall down into the depths, unnoticed. The people around me were laughing and chatting, and most of them got off the car at the first or second stop, there were only a few of us who continued on to the last stop at the summit.

It was a cloudless day, I saw the vacationers at the telescopes through which one could observe the range of the Alps as far as Bernina and even Mont Blanc, I remained off to the side, the people dispersed on the platform, no one was looking in my direction, I climbed over the railing and jumped onto the snow-covered rock scarcely two meters below me. I quickly headed toward the crest from the station and looked around after a minute. I had remained unnoticed.

I reached the crest quickly, I left it behind me, the mountains that I had seen every day, the valley with its villages, all that had disappeared, already nearly forgotten, a new landscape unfolded, first a small snowfield, behind it a new, unknown ridge, mountain ranges all the way to the distant horizon, and patches of forest down below. No cable could be seen any more, no steel supports, no houses. Terrible and invigorating, a great solitude opened up before me. I walked in a northerly direction from that point with the intention of keeping approximately the same altitude. I did not want to go down, so whenever the terrain forced me to descend, I tried to regain the height right away, which was easy to do. The sky was a deep absorbing blue.

I paid no attention to the position of the sun. I first noticed evening approaching as the cold drifted in from the lengthening shadows. I didn't get cold, I felt comfortable in my sturdy clothes and shoes, even the weight of my knapsack, which had some food in it, made me feel content, stars began to shine, big and motionless above me. I sat down in a hollow in the next rock face, ate some of my provisions, and quickly fell asleep.

The next days passed in the same way. I crossed the mountains, I felt no boredom, no weariness, no fear. It also didn't surprise me that I met no one, I had no desire to meet anyone, the mountains were deserted. The silent movement of the air, the play of light on a gnarled tree far below me, the soaring of a distant bird of prey were enough for me.

I didn't know how much time had passed when I reached the foothills. The high walls receded, wooded hills appeared, a bay of the sea opened wide before me. On its banks, as if through a magnifying glass, I saw a city in the distance, in the shadow of a thicket a farmer was plowing; not far from him the shepherd stood with his staff, just as I had seen him as a child in the mountains. Over the foaming water sails swelled, the foot of someone sinking flashed briefly, and on the horizon a rayless sun was going down.

But soon the light changed. I had now climbed down farther, the sinking sun had disappeared behind the rocks, the sea was no longer visible either; only an inlet, almost separated from the main body of water by long tongues of land and by a remote range of mountains, extended far into the foreground, resembling a peaceful lake with a few evening fishermen on it. The light had taken on the soft, overpowering blue that had surrounded me in the arena of Padua, toward the horizon it gradually turned a wistful pink, and above drifted a chain of clouds, lit from the top by white rays; on the ground the light flashed golden between the shadows cast by mighty treetops onto the clearing. Men and women sat in unmoving, reflective calm, half-naked or clothed in red, white, yellow robes, in two or three groups in the glade, behind which rose a small castle on the left. I felt the mild wind, I heard a whispering, a voice repeated: Always, always, always . . . perhaps it was my own, the stillness entered into me, I had become a part of it.

Stephan Hermlin was born in 1915 in Chemnitz (now Karl-Marx-Stadt) in Saxony and grew up in Berlin, the son of a German-Jewish industrialist and an English mother. In 1931 he joined the Communist Youth Organization, and after Hitler's seizure of power in 1933 he went underground to fight the fascist regime. In 1936 he emigrated first to Egypt, then Palestine and England, finally joining the Republican forces in Spain. During World War II he fought in the French Resistance and published his first poems in Switzerland. He returned to Germany in 1945 to work with Hans Mayer and Golo Mann at the Hessian Broadcasting Company in Frankfurt am Main. In 1947 he settled in East Berlin.

Hermlin is a member of the Socialist Unity Party and the Writers Union of the GDR, and Vice President of PEN International. He was formerly secretary in charge of poetry for the East Berlin Academy of Arts, from which post he was relieved in 1963 because he provided a forum for unorthodox poets. A staunch supporter of young authors, he is credited with discovering Sarah Hirsch and poet and songwriter Wolf Biermann. In defense of so-called deviant writers he has said that "a poet must have the right to dream irrationally." In 1976 he was among the first to protest when Biermann was stripped of his East German citizenship while on a reading tour in West Germany. In 1979, when a new list of writers was proposed for expulsion from the Writers Union (which would make it impossible for their work to be published), Hermlin was the only member who dared oppose the Union's president, Hermann Kant, with a plea on behalf of the threatened writers. When in 1978 party secretary Konrad Naumann characterized Biermann and his supporters as "bourgeois artists," Hermlin responded at the East German Writers Congress by saying: "A writer who does not know his roots, the tradition in which he stands, cannot assume a firm stance in the struggles of his time... I am a late bourgeois writer—what else could I be as a writer."

Familiar with many languages, Hermlin has translated the work of many poets, including Aragon, Eluard, Neruda, Nazim Hikmet, and many American poets. His own work includes poetry, essays, and fiction. This is his first book to be translated into English.

The typefaces used in this book are 12-point Aldus Roman and Italic, designed in 1954 by Hermann Zapf for D. Stempel, Frankfurt, based on Renaissance models.